More Praise for *The Seven Paths*

"There is much to learn from any person who has lived his life trying to heed the wisdom he has gathered from the lingering voices of his ancestors—especially in an age, like our own, when those voices have been spurned. Ezekiel Sanchez (Good Buffalo Eagle), cofounder of ANASAZI Foundation, is such a person. He has used the ancient, tested wisdom of his people to touch the souls of thousands of once-troubled young people and their families and show them the way to reunion and peace. Such a person also is his literary collaborator, Jim Ferrell. In *The Seven Paths*, they have distilled their unique and luminous insight. Reading this book receptively, you will likely catch yourself already forward walking in your heart and awakening to the light."
—**C. Terry Warner, PhD, founder, The Arbinger Institute**

"This book is profound! The principle of 'We' is the secret to every success on and off the field."
—**Steve Young, NFL Hall of Fame quarterback and ESPN commentator**

"Through the story of the Seven Paths, my daughter realized how she, too, had walked backward, away from her family. This profound discovery saved my daughter's life, which in turn saved our entire family. It gave her a solid foundation to navigate through her very difficult teenage years...it gave our lost child new feet to find her way—her path to becoming a loving, successful young adult with truly a heart at peace."
—**Elaine Taylor, President, The Taylor Family Foundation**

"Speaking with the wisdom of ancient ones, this guide to life's challenging journey is brilliantly accessible and spiritually transforming."
—**Richard Ferre, MD, adolescent and adult psychiatrist**

"*The Seven Paths* lays the groundwork for personal growth, insights, and strength required in long-term recovery."
—**Jon Memmott, retired judge**

"Every page is filled with insight and share it, and read it again."
—**Dale Tingey, PhD, founder and Ex**
Services

D0967455

"*The Seven Paths* epitomizes the strength of one of my favorite words: TEAM—Together Everyone Achieves More."
—**Bart Starr, NFL Hall of Fame quarterback**

"In the universal moments of feeling stuck or lost, the Seven Paths are simple and profound truths that provide not only solace but genuine ways to change your heart."
—**Courtney Merrill, LMFT, marriage and family therapist and educational consultant**

"ANASAZI Foundation's *Seven Paths* illustrates an oft-forgotten truth that it is not our experiences that determine the quality of our lives but who we are morally when we pass through those experiences. To walk in the light instead of in darkness means we see our experiences truthfully and learn and grow. When we betray the light within us, we walk in darkness and we find our experiences burdensome. This book is an invitation to all to live truthfully and distinguish toxic from nourishing ways of being in the world."
—**Terrance D. Olson, PhD, Ernest Osborne award winner in Family Life Education**

"*The Seven Paths* is truly a blessing. I recommend it to anyone in need of healing, wisdom, power, and goodness."
—**Stan Block, MD, author and founder, Mind-Body Bridging**

"A little book with a *big* message! *The Seven Paths* reminds us of who we are, our relationship to our Creator, and how happiness with our families is within our grasp."
—**Danny Ainge, former professional basketball and baseball player and President of Basketball Operations, Boston Celtics**

"It is a privilege to recommend *The Seven Paths*. ANASAZI is one of the best programs for helping young people and adults make major changes in their lives, and I am thrilled this book will make the philosophy and wisdom its program is based on accessible to a larger audience."
—**Ralph H. Earle, MDiv, PhD, founder and President, Psychological Counseling Services, Ltd.**

The Seven Paths

The Seven Paths

Changing One's Way of Walking in the World

ANASAZI Foundation

Foreword by Good Buffalo Eagle

Berrett–Koehler Publishers, Inc.
a BK Life book

Berrett-Koehler Publishers, Inc.
1333 Broadway, Suite 1000
Oakland, CA 94612-1921
Tel: (510) 817-2277   Fax: (510) 817-2278   www.bkconnection.com

Ordering Information
Quantity sales. Special discounts are available on quantity purchases by corporations, associations, and others. For details, contact the "Special Sales Department" at the Berrett-Koehler address above.
Individual sales. Berrett-Koehler publications are available through most bookstores. They can also be ordered directly from Berrett-Koehler:
Tel: (800) 929-2929; Fax: (802) 864-7626; www.bkconnection.com
Orders for college textbook/course adoption use. Please contact Berrett-Koehler: Tel: (800) 929-2929; Fax: (802) 864-7626.
Orders by U.S. trade bookstores and wholesalers. Please contact Ingram Publisher Services, Tel: (800) 509-4887; Fax: (800) 838-1149; E-mail: customer.service@ingrampublisherservices.com; or visit www.ingram publisherservices.com/Ordering for details about electronic ordering.

Berrett-Koehler and the BK logo are registered trademarks of Berrett-Koehler Publishers, Inc.

Printed in the United States of America.

Berrett-Koehler books are printed on long-lasting acid-free paper. When it is available, we choose paper that has been manufactured by environmentally responsible processes. These may include using trees grown in sustainable forests, incorporating recycled paper, minimizing chlorine in bleaching, or recycling the energy produced at the paper mill.

Library of Congress Cataloging-in-Publication Data
Good Buffalo Eagle.
  The seven paths : changing one's way of walking in the world / Good Buffalo Eagle.
    pages cm
  ISBN 978-1-60994-919-8 (pbk.)
  1. Indians of North America—Religion. 2. Indian philosophy—North America. 3. Mind and body. 4. Spiritual life. I. Title.
  E98.R3G666 213
  299.7—dc23   2013015200

First Edition
22 21 20 19 18 17 16   10 9 8 7 6 5 4 3 2

Copyeditor: Elissa Rabellino
Interior design, composition, and production management: Leigh McLellan Design
Cover/jacket designer: Nicole Hayward
Cover art and illustrations: Lehi Sanchez

Contents

Earth

Dedication

*Most sincerely, we thank the young people
and their families who have come
to walk the trail with us.
It is to you that we dedicate this book.
Your courage and love give this book
life and meaning. Your forward
walking has filled the world with beauty.
One of our TrailWalkers,
Lara Ackerman, summed it up
when she said,*

*"The most beautiful thing in the world
is a heart that is changing."*

Foreword

I am Good Buffalo Eagle. Hear my words.

The Creator gave all Two-Legged beings a sacred gift. We call this the Gift of Choice. Regardless of where we are born, all come to earth with this gift. Along with this Gift of Choice, all Two-Legged beings have a sense of knowing right from wrong from the One Who Stands Within. Therefore, the Gift of Choice allows us to choose knowingly.

My Pauline, the Woman of my Heart, states that in her Navajo language, life is a walking, a journey. So, if life upon Mother Earth is a journey, there are two ways to walk.

By applying the Gift of Choice, we can choose to walk forward or we can choose to walk backward. Because we choose knowingly, with every step we take forward or backward, we are accountable.

Because we are accountable, there are consequences. Consequences, however, are not chosen. They might be delayed, but by and by they will come.

Forward Walking choices are rewarded with consequences that light the way to peace, happiness, joy, comfort, knowledge, and wisdom. Backward Walking choices bring to the Two-Legged beings consequences of misery, despair, and darkness.

At the end of our lives, when our bodies are about to be laid in Mother Earth, we will know for ourselves whether we are a Two-Legged being full of light or a Two-Legged being full of darkness. At that time, we cannot turn around and point a finger accusingly in the air. WE will know because WE are the ones who chose to walk forward toward the light or backward toward darkness.

Hear my words. Ponder the narrative of the Seven Paths. For you, like the young man in the story, can turn toward a New Beginning. Don't believe the dark whisperings that invite you to walk backward. At any time in your life, you have the power to turn forward. No matter how young or old you are, you have the power to turn and walk forward. That's the ANASAZI Way.

We extend an invitation to all to utilize the power of the Gift of Choice, which will teach us the Forward Walkings that will bring peace. Let's look at the present and with anticipation into the future at what we can become—a Two-Legged being full of light!

I am Good Buffalo Eagle. I have spoken.

Preface

There is much to be learned from the world around us—far more than we normally comprehend. The Ancient Ones knew this well—most particularly the wise teachers among them—those who, in the Navajo tongue, were called "Anasazi."

These ancient teachers understood well that no man is as wise as Mother Earth. She has witnessed every human day, every human struggle, every human pain, and every human joy. For maladies of both body and spirit, the wise ones of old pointed man to the hills. For man too is of the dust and Mother Earth stands ready to nurture and heal her children.

Unfortunately, modern man has moved far from Mother Earth. And as he has done so, his maladies have multiplied. Our work is with those who have been struck with the maladies of the modern age. We have found that no modern prescriptions heal the human heart so fully or so well as the prescription of the Ancient Ones. "To the hills," they would say. To which we would add, "To the trees, the valleys, and the streams, as well." For there is a power in nature that man has ignored. And the result has been heartache and pain.

This book, *The Seven Paths*, presents what might be described as a way to healing—seven elements among nature that combine to heal human hearts. It is a way designed by the Creator and presented by Mother Earth to all who have the wisdom to seek her. We have learned to seek her often over these many years, and like the Anasazi of old, we have the sacred trust of inviting others to do the same.

Beginnings

The Making of a Walking

The Age of "I"

I am a lone voice, a lone man,

the last of a people.

In my walking, I have seen many days of the earth—
from the days of dust and simple villages to the
days of concrete and gleaming cities.

I have observed revolutions
in science, medicine, and technology.

I have watched as man, once bound to the earth,
has launched himself toward the stars.

I have seen what I never could have imagined and
what my people never could have dreamed of.

Man has become impressive indeed.

But, young friend (and no matter your age, to me you
are young), of all the days I have witnessed, today—
your day—is the most unhappy.

I see it in the faces I meet on sidewalks and in the voices
I hear in your cities.

Mother Earth has never been more crowded,
yet her inhabitants have never been more lonely.

You live in the age of "I." Man looks out for himself, and only secondarily for others. In the philosophy of your day, happiness is a product of the fulfillment of personal wants.

Would it surprise you to hear that man's unhappiness is due in large measure to the way he is seeking after happiness?

You know this already from your own life.
For when you have been unhappy, you have been unhappy *with others*—with your father or mother, your sister or brother, your spouse, your son, your daughter.
If unhappiness is *with* others, wouldn't it stand to reason that happiness must be *with others* as well?

Man's obsession with his *own* wants is taking him further from those without whom happiness cannot be found.

It is taking him from his people.

In truth, it is taking him from his true self.

Away from My People

I was once known among my people as
"The WE walking lost."

A strange way of speaking, to your ear, no doubt.

And a way I once thought strange as well.

For the speaking of my people had not yet become mine.

You see, there is no "I" alone in the speaking of our people.

When referring to another among us, as when
referring to ourselves, we speak in "WE."

One day, while on a hunt with others who
were earning their early merits of manhood,
the village leader's son—once my friend
but by then my rival—claimed my kill as his own.

Both of us rushed to the fallen carcass.

"You!" I yelled, violating our language's
commitment to community, "You lie!"

Others in the party rushed to pull us off each other.
I swung at him in vain, restrained by the others behind me.

We were taken before the village council,
my father sitting among them.

My rival's father rose, looking back and forth from
me to his son. He stood silently for several minutes.
Finally he said, "WE suffered today. Our warring in
the forest was against Our way. WE do not fight WE."

"But WE," I interrupted, pointing at the other, "is cheating
WE!" I said, looking first at the chief and then at my father.

But my father looked at me in stone silence.
He offered nothing—no defense, not even a look
of encouragement or understanding.

My heart was wounded.

My rival's father now focused his eyes on me.

"WE, young son," he said slowly, "have much to learn.
Much to learn before manhood."

"What about WE!" I exclaimed, pointing at his son.
"Does not WE have much to learn, too?"

The air stood still in the chamber.

"Silence," he said with a quiet firmness.
"Silence is what WE must learn."

I turned and fled in humiliation and fury—
my father's silence closing my heart and
my rival's air of triumph poking at my skin.

From that moment on,
I began to turn my heart from my people.

I resented the village elders, especially my father. And I kept
myself distant from those who had before been friends.

The mere thought of my rival stirred my heart to anger.

And our beliefs and customs irritated my ears.

I saw pain in my people's faces when I mocked our ways and reveled in what I considered victory. But my bitterness grew.

My parents bothered me, my sisters and my brother bothered me, my village bothered me.

I longed to be independent and free— free from the tyranny of WE.

And so one morning, long before the dawn, I ran.

My People, Again

But I discovered a surprising thing in my running:

Those who had granted me life and language accompanied
me wherever I went. I thought with words they taught me.
Their very identity was replicated in my skin.

Although I had left them physically, they nevertheless
traveled with me in my mind, my flesh, my heart.

How surprised I was to discover this—
that there was no escaping my life.

With a heart that glared at my people, I glared as well
at the hill that rose inconveniently before me.

I swung angrily at the tree that obstructed my way.

I cursed at the valley that fell far below me.

I shook my fists at the rapids in the stream.

When I finally scratched my way to the summit of
Big Mountain and turned for a final glance at the village
in the distance, I was committed to never returning.

But you know that I did return, for you have sensed
the reverence and love I now have for my people.

And perhaps you have guessed that I desire
nothing more than to be among them again.

How did it happen? What brought me home
and taught me love and reverence?

How did I discover happiness with a people
from whom I had felt estranged, even banished?

My young friend,
this is what I have pondered every day since.

And the answer may surprise you.

The hill, the tree, the valley, and the stream—
those objects of my wrath—were my teachers.

Mother Earth reintroduced me to my people.

Nature as Teacher

Unfortunately, modern man has become
so focused on harnessing nature's resources
that he has forgotten how to learn from them.

If you let them, however, the elements of nature
will teach you as they have taught me.

Consider:

What was the point in being angry at the hills?
They had nothing against me.

And how silly to curse the trees when they merely offered
me shade. Likewise the valleys that offered rest, and the
streams refreshment . . . what cause had I to blame them?

Mother Earth taught me that my anger
toward nature was unfounded.

And she therefore invited me to open my heart to this
possibility: so too may be my anger toward man.

Forward and Backward Walking

In the years since, I have learned that
the point of life's walk is not where or how far
I move my feet but how I am moved in my heart.

If I walk far but am angry toward others as I journey,
I walk nowhere.

If I conquer mountains but hold grudges against others
as I climb, I conquer nothing.

If I see much but regard others as enemies, I see no one.

My young friend, when the days of your walking begin
to draw to a close, you will know that I speak the truth.

Whether we walk among our people or alone
among the hills, happiness in life's walking depends
on how we feel about others in our hearts.

We travel only as far and as high as our hearts will take us.

When I ran from my people, *this* is what the hills,
the trees, the valleys, and the streams invited me to learn—
and before it was too late:

That the success of my journey depended on
whether my heart walked forward—*toward* my people—
instead of backward, *away from* them.

My walk is nearly finished. Soon I will join my people.

How fortunate and grateful I am that I want to.

My young friend, before the close of my days,

I will share the making of my walking—paths of clarity
and healing that can be found among the hills.

May your heart walk forward in your receiving.

1

The Path of Light

A Ray of Light

A few days into my journey, still kicking against nature,
I swung at what turned out to be poison oak.

I cursed my carelessness and
my anticipated discomfort and pain.

Truly all creation is against me, I murmured.

❧

Later that day, I tripped in a bone-dry creek bed,
smashing my knee against a rock.
I remember grimacing in pain toward an empty sky.

As I lay there, I recalled words my father had spoken to me
while on a hunt: "WE who lose our footing have lost our
way," he had said. "Our walking is in darkness."

❧

What did he mean by walking in darkness? I wondered, as
I picked myself up and limped on my way. *And what did
darkness have to do with stumbling in daylight?*

❧

Despite my anger toward my father, in that moment I had to
accept that I had seen my father, and the great ones among
our people, sure-footed and rooted upon the earth as any
tree or plant, yet as light as a seed upon the wind.

This memory awakened my life to light
and for a moment brightened a son's hurting heart.

Light and Darkness

Young friend, each morning offers lessons in light.
For the morning light teaches the most basic of truths:

Light chases away darkness.

*

We order our physical lives by this truth, for good reason.
Our own instruments of sight, our eyes,
mislead and are weak in the dark.

We need help from above
if we are to make progress in our journeys.

So we begin each day's walk after the great light
illuminates the terrain around us.

In this, we are wise in the walking of our feet.

*

But, young friend, are we as wise in the walking of the heart?

Do you and I allow light to
chase darkness from our *souls* as well?

This was the meaning of my father's saying.
Darkness *within* clouds the world *without*.

*

Perhaps I stumbled in the creek bed because
I was too troubled on the inside to see with clarity.

And maybe I failed to recognize the poison oak
because I had turned my heart from the light.

In hills, as well as in villages and cities, hazards
and predators find those who walk backward.

*

My young friend, having seen your day
and the dangers that lurk in its shadows,
I repeat the words that first pointed me toward light:

"WE who lose the light within have lost our way."

I ask you:

Does your heart walk forward in the light?

Illumination of the Heart

My own answer to that question has been,
"Sometimes yes and sometimes no."

But after many days of hating my life amid the hills,
I began to welcome the dawn—and the trees, valleys,
and streams that were illuminated by it.

I could feel my heart walking farther and my feet stepping
with more assurance upon the earth.

Just as the morning light sweeps away the night, the darkness
within me began to be chased away by a dawn in my soul.

Then and many times since, my body and my heart have
been illuminated alike—each of them saved by a sun.

❦

Young friend, have you felt what I am speaking of?

Have you felt light in your soul?

Have you felt warmth where before was coldness?

Have you discovered insight where
before you had been blind?

❦

As great as is the light above us,
greater by far is the light within.

❦

The outward light is but a reflection of the inner.

The Source of the Light

I know the source of this light.

During my days of solitude, I have come to know Him well.

❦

"Him?" you ask.

Yes, *Him*.

I speak of the Creator. He has walked with me often
in my journeys, and it has been by learning to walk
with Him that I have learned to walk forward.

❦

Are you surprised by my candor?

In a world that has killed the sacred,
mention of it can seem shocking, even foolhardy.

But how foolhardy it is to kill the sacred!

And how shocking to think that we could!

❦

For there is always a light that walks forward.

When I was very young, I played in that light;
I learned to play walking forward. I know this must be so,
for I loved those I played with.

For even in my darkest hour, when love was far from me,
he who is light walked near.

How do I know?

Because of what I have already mentioned—
because of the dawns in my soul.

Darkness cannot illuminate itself any more than
night can call itself day.

Light means that the sun is near.

The dawns I have felt in my soul testify that
I am known by the Giver of light.

To walk forward, I need only walk where he shows me.

Messengers of the Light

All creation shows us how to follow the Creator's light.

Look around and learn.

*

Notice how the hills receive the dawn.
They feel no attachment to darkness.
As quickly as the sun rises, the darkness from them flees.

You will witness the same response in the trees,
the valleys, and the streams.

*

And notice as well that all nature flourishes in the light.

The hills and the trees reach to greet it.
The grasses in the valleys grow tall and green
under its influence. The stream shimmers and
multiplies the light to all that are around it.

*

In the early days of my running, nature's acceptance
of the light stood in stark contrast to my own. For I had
turned my back to the light—my thoughts and feelings
withering in bitterness, so centered on myself that I had
neither thought nor desire to reflect on others.

But the elements of nature were never offended
by the back that I turned. They still reached,
they still shimmered, they still grew.

By so doing, they kept inviting me to turn again to
the light—to join them in stretching forth my arms,
brightening my thoughts, and conversing again with *others*.

In these and other ways, the hills, the trees, the valleys,
and the streams testify of the Creator and his walking.

If you listen, you will hear them do so,
for his voice can be heard in them.

It is a beckoning voice—
a voice that calls us to walk forward.

A voice that brightens both soil and soul.

A voice that invites us to join him.

2

The Path of Wind

A Voice on the Wind

Weeks into my journey, I came to the edge of a land
known by my people as "the land of winding cliffs."

Sandstone ridges filled the horizon.
Junipers peeked out from crags in the rocky cliffs,
but otherwise vegetation seemed scarce.

✦

I had never seen this land, but I had heard rumor of it
among my people. It was said to be a place to be avoided—
a confusing land where many entered and few returned.

But here it was, too immense to be avoided, or so I thought.
And so I entered it, despite my people's warnings.

✦

For most of a day, I carefully picked my way from one
canyon to the next, consulting the sun above for direction.
But as the day grew longer, I became less sure of each choice.

By the time the sun set, I was lost.
Rock walls rose high on either side, obscuring
the night sky and pressing their shadows against me.
After a series of choices I could not retrace, I found myself
stuck in a labyrinth of dead ends and gullies.

It was the last time in my life that I would feel fear.

✦

Yes, the last time.

For as morning dawn broke,
I discovered a truth that casts fear away:

I discovered, as my people have always known,
that I was not alone.

◆

I heard something. Or perhaps it is better to say that
I *felt* something—a stir in the still air around me.

It was faint at first, almost imperceptible.

But as I tuned myself to it, the stir became a voice—
its echo traveling the bends to me,
bringing comfort to my soul.

◆

Although separated yet by a great distance, the voice
connected me to One who would save me.

His voice became my companion—
a guide who showed me the safe way forward.

◆

Even when I thought I was most alone,
I was connected to Him . . . by the wind.

The Breath of Life

How foolish I was to think that I had ever been alone.

And how haughty.

As if *I* had created the air that had given me breath.

I heard the voice on the wind in the moment
I realized I couldn't survive on my own.

And as I hearkened to that voice, I learned gratitude.

My gratitude started with the most basic of realizations:
I was grateful to be alive.

And what I learned among the winding cliffs was
that my life was not mine alone but another's.

My life had been *given* to me.

The voice that saved me and the wind
that carried it to me were gifts. Yes, gifts.

I had spent my life taking all but myself for granted—

I had insisted on going my own way,

I had ignored warnings and
entered the land of winding cliffs,

I had made my condition hopeless.

Yet the wind still sustained my every breath,
lengthening my life so that I might discover
the voice that saves.

✒

My young friend, I hope it doesn't take despair
for you to realize: The air that sustains us, like the light
that warms us, is a gift from the Creator.

To breathe is to breathe his breath.

The air that sustains our existence is a testimony of his.

The Connection of Nature

This gift from above connects all creation.

Look around and you will see that I speak the truth.
But you must look with more than your eyes,
for they deceive. You must look with your soul.

❧

The hills, the trees, the valleys, the streams—
they appear to be separate and disconnected,
lone elements pieced together to make a landscape.

But that is because man measures connectedness
only by what can be seen with the eye.

❧

The winding cliffs taught me of a deeper connectedness—
a connection not so much seen as heard or felt.

It is this: The edge of the stream is not its banks,
the beginning of the hill is not its slope, the hem of the tree
is not its branch. All reach out and unite on the wind.

❧

My young friend, close your eyes and you will see the truth
in my words. You perceive the stream before you arrive at
its waters. You feel the presence of the hills before you reach
their slopes. You hear the trees before they give you shade.

Your presence as well is delivered to all around you
far in advance of your bodily arrival.

For the space between the elements of nature is not empty.
It is occupied to the full—occupied by the air that joins us.

To walk is to press your presence into all you walk among.
And to feel the press of their presence in return.

Like the saving voice of my deliverer,
your presence spreads far beyond you.

It walks—forward or backward—upon the wind.

The Connection of Man

You know the connection of which I speak.

You have known it since your birth.

For nature's connection is but a hint of man's.

#

You are no more separate from your family and friends
than are nature's elements around you.

How do I know?

Because although they've been gone for many years,
to this day I feel the breeze of my mother, the firm wind
of my father, the gusts of my sisters and brother.

Their lives and mine still mingle in my soul.

#

My young friend, I wish I could put my arm around you
and look you in the eye to help you understand.

My life was never merely mine. Nor is your life merely yours.

We owe our lives to others.

And in our daily living, we live *together*, connected with
the people around us. They occupy our thoughts and inform
our feelings, and we speak their words through our lips.

We are ever conversing, even through our silence.

For our hearts are ever sending messages upon the wind.

Messages on the Wind

There is a legend about the wind that I wish you to know.

It is said that the wind has a spirit of its own.
This is why it can move around Mother Earth.

As it moves around the earth, the wind carries within it
the words uttered by the lips and hearts of every man,
woman, and child. Every laugh, every sad sigh,
every joyful sound, every foul word, every song . . .

It is said that the wind carries these words
and sounds in its bosom until the last day,
when we stand, with the wind, before the Creator.

At that day, the wind will unlock the words of our lips and hearts,
and we will hear the messages that we have sent upon it.

It is said that at that time, our messages will bring us
deep joy or bitter sadness.

Soon, I will see that day.

But already I am a witness of the legend.

For I have heard the sounds of man upon the wind,
and my heart has been made sometimes happy and
sometimes sad for what I have heard.

But there is more to the legend, my young friend.
And it is this that I wish you most to remember.

Our hearts, and their messages, can change.

As we stand before the Creator, we will be saddened or
made joyful by the messages still spoken by our hearts.

So, my young friend, when the morning dawn breaks,
let your heart be filled with grateful words
for your daily walking.

Happiness itself depends on it.

3

The Path of Water

The Need for Water

I escaped the land of winding cliffs to the south.
. And when I did so, I changed course from where
I initially had planned to go.

From that day, I no longer ran from my people
but merely persisted in staying away from them.

Days passed into months and months into years.

I grew into manhood without the companionship of
my father and without the worrying comfort of my mother.

The hills and the valleys raised me.

ᒧ

Then, as well as now, in my daily walking, I have sought
the answer to one question above all others:

Where will I find water?

ᒧ

Think about water for a moment.

Have you ever considered all it does for us?

I have learned to walk near water, for beside it the earth
springs forth to provide shade and refreshment.

I try to rest near water,
for I need it for nourishment and strength.

I bathe in water, for it cleanses and invigorates my skin.

My final destination at the end of each day has been
a pool of pure water.

And when traveling in dry places, each morning
I have set off with as much of that pool as I could carry.

For I have learned from dry journeys that deserts can be
weathered only by those who are sustained by deep waters.

I know, for I have stumbled and fallen facedown
on the desert floor, my throat unable to swallow,
my eyes unable to see.

I know the feeling of walking too long without water.
I have felt the thirsty fingers of death constricting
around my soul.

As is common with so much in life, I failed to understand
how much I needed water until I was without it.

Drought in the Soul

I say this not to scare but to warn.

Perhaps you too wander in deserts as I have,
unaware of your own perilous lack of water.

◆

Don't misunderstand. I speak not so much of
where feet walk as where hearts walk.

The deserts and lush forests *around* us mirror
the deserts and lush forests *within*.

◆

Our bodies, like the earth, can be parched and thirsty.

And both point to the thirst of the soul.

Moisture to the Soul

Let me tell you of *my* thirst.

Or rather, let me tell you of my *recovery* from thirst, and with
it the desire for life that I rediscovered through water.

◊

I wish I could say that I entered the wilderness because of
my love for nature, but you know this wouldn't be the truth.

A lone existence in the wilderness seemed my only option
when I set my back against my people.

◊

Over a period of months, the reasons for my flight,
so upsettingly clear to me then, gradually faded from
my heart—or, should I say, were washed from it.
For as I look back, I believe it was water, more than
anything else, that cleansed my soul.

Although I was angry with all creation—cursing at every hill,
swinging at every tree, reviling every valley, kicking at every
stream—try as I might, I couldn't stay mad at the water.

◊

I tried, oh how I tried—for I hated life itself.
But every day, by bending to the stream to take a drink,
I was nevertheless choosing to live.

Think of it. The cool drinks refreshed my body, to be sure. But more powerful by far was the refreshment to my soul.

◊

The life that I had hated I now thirsted to save.

And with each saving drink, those who had given me life seemed more worthy of salvation as well.

Water was moistening my heart.

Water's Lessons

Water moistened my heart as I observed the way it
moistened the earth.

◊

I observed how water produced green shade
in abundance all along its length,
giving comfortable cover from the scorching sun.

In comparison, I began to realize that the banks in my soul
were barren. I could tell, for I felt little respite from the
bitter feelings that burned within me—thought of my rival
still stirred resentment within me, and I continued to carry
grudges toward my father and our people.

There was no abundance in my soul
because my heart had run dry.

◊

I observed as well that water would not scar.
As quickly as I removed my foot, my hand,
or my spear from its heart, water washed away
the wound and made itself whole.

My soul, on the other hand, bore scars aplenty.
I preserved each painful scar in its original state,
like ancient images chiseled in stone,
as evidence of others' guilt.

◊

But every day, water taught me of another way.

Water's mission is not to preserve hurt but to wash it away.
And not only to clear the earth of strife, but to combine
with air and light to grow beauty in its place.

◊

If ever there walked a man who needed water to work its
miracle in his heart, it was me. As I ran from my people,
my soul was cankered and dying. I needed water
to bring me back to life.

Each day's search for water to refresh and cleanse
my body became as well a search for water that
would refresh and cleanse my soul.

◊

When I found it, I couldn't believe I had been so blind.

Water's Source

One year, at the height of the dry season, I encountered
a storm such as I have never experienced before or since.

Water poured from the heavens, filling the air
so completely that it was even difficult for me to catch
my breath. Within minutes, what had been
parched earth had become a raging river of sliding soil.

The earth was giving way all around me
and threatening to sweep me away in its fury.

I looked for shelter but could find none.
Trees were defenseless against the weight of the storm,
and my buckskin, which I had tried to secure as a barrier,
was snatched away by the torrent.

Instinctively I clawed my way up a gentle, stony slope.
I had been in that area for some time and knew
the feature well—a slight dome in the earth that traveled
in both directions as far as the eye could see.

The stone provided a foundation for my feet, and
with the storm tearing at me, I started to run with all my
strength in the direction of the land of my people.

◊

I am not an emotional man.
Or at least, I had not been until that night.
But as I ran, I cried tears as thick as the rain about me.

I ran all night and into the next morning
until finally the storm broke.

Light poured through the parting clouds above me,
expelling the shadows from the earth. I lifted my eyes
in the direction that I had been running in.

Far in the distance I could make out a faint shape
against the sky, an outline that would never have been
visible but for the clear, post-torrential air.

It was a mountain. Not just any mountain,
but a mountain I had been avoiding for ages.

I was looking from far away at the summit of
Big Mountain—the last place from which
I had seen my people.

I bowed my head in silence.

Water, which had been soothing me
for months and years, had finally healed my heart.
My tears had brought me home.

The rain had resurrected from deep within me
the desire to be with my people.

◊

I looked heavenward. The rain had fallen from
where the sun now shone. It was then that I knew:

The water that cleanses the heart comes
from the same place as the sun that lightens it.

Water, too, is a gift from above.

4

The Path of Stone

The Wisdom of Stone

I mentioned that on the night of the great storm I found
safe passage on a formation of stone—one of many times
that stone has supported, taught, or saved me.

Taught? you might wonder. *Stone teaches?*

Yes.

Every stone we observe has been on the earth for ages.
Should we be surprised if they possess wisdom
that we do not?

In the months and years I was separated from my people,
wisdom was at my feet all the while.

The stones that met my every step—
those silent patriarchs from years past—
they made wisdom my foundation.
Or at least offered to do so.

To become wise, I had to learn to hear their silence.

The Foundation of Peace

Initially, I heard stone only when I turned to it
for help—as when I needed to cross a stream
or when I desired to shape a tool.

But even when I have ignored it, stone has always
offered itself to me and supported my every step.

What has stone offered?

In a word:

Peace.

Why peace?

Because amid turmoil, such as during the great storm,
stone has offered me safe passage.

When the earth has seemed to be shifting around me,
stone has been my sure foundation.

When my own meager abilities have left me
desperate and wanting, stone has offered its hand,
allowing me to fashion weapons, utensils,
and tools that have given me the means to live.

I speak of stone's gift to the body, yes.
But only to teach you of stone's gift to the soul.

For just as the outer light points to an inner,

just as the wind carries the thoughts of my heart,

just as water cleanses my soul as well as my skin,

so the stone underfoot points to something within.

My young friend, consider your life and
you will find evidence for what I am saying.

You can probably remember times when you have felt
unsteady even when the ground beneath you was solid.
And other times when perhaps you have felt
sure-footed and at peace no matter the terrain.

The stone that has supported my feet has taught me
of a greater stone—a stone that has weathered every calamity
and that can therefore support me in mine.

In my walking, I have discovered a stone
that supports the heart.

Every forward step of my walking has been
a step on the path of that stone.

To Be as a Stone

You will find this sure stone as you become
as the stones that help you in your journey.

Don't make the mistake that I made in my early walking—
to look down on the stones. They are noble.

Early in my running, I ignored them. Now I revere them.
Occasionally I would curse them. Now I praise them.

To be as a stone . . . that is a worthy goal indeed.

I say this in all seriousness.

Don't be offended by the stone that turns beneath
your feet. After all, the stone isn't offended by you,
even though you were the one who turned it.

Do you appreciate the willingness of the stones to support
you even when you try your best to hurt them?

Do you notice their willingness to help you even
after you have failed to notice them?

Are you awed that they offer the same help to
all who walk by, over, and on them?

Are you touched by their humility and patience?

Are you instructed by the way they warm to the light?

To be as a stone.

Yes. That has become the desire of my heart.

Forward and Backward
Use of Stone

Don't misunderstand.

The world thinks of stone as something cold,
something hard, something unforgiving.

That is what stone seems like in the dark—when *we* are cold,
hard, and unforgiving. *And* when we witness the damage
that can be done with stone when it is wielded by those
whose hearts are cold, hard, and unforgiving.

But stone is very different in the light.

Those who walk forward use stone as well, but they use it
to help, not to injure—to create, not to destroy.

Our understanding, regard, and use for stone
depends on our walking:

Walk forward in the light, and stone will be
the means of delivering peace.

Walk backward in the darkness, and it will
be the means of making war.

When I saw this in stone, I saw my reflection in the rocks.

For *I* sometimes bring peace and sometimes make war.

Stone is what I make of it.

Stone is but an extension of *me*.

Stone's Question

As I have read on stone walls the stories
of those who have gone before,

as I have added my own stories for those
who would come after,

as I have used stone to reshape Mother Earth . . .

I have come to hear from stone a question.

Yes, a question.

Don't be misled by the silence.
It is merely stone's patient wait for your answer.

Here is stone's question:

What impressions and depressions will you leave
on the people around you?

Like the sharpest stones, our words, our actions,
our attitudes—all wield influence.

They engrave stories in the hearts of others.

We engrave those stories with our own hearts.
For whatever we do on the outside,
people know how we feel about them in our hearts.

So stone asks this question:

Do we invite peace or provoke war?

Do we walk backward, scarring the landscape
with jagged hearts, or do we walk forward on
the stone path that is the foundation of peace—
inviting others, by our peaceful walk, to join us?

5

The Path of Plants

The Secret of Plants

For all who have a desire to change their walking,
nature displays in abundance the way to do it.

The answer grows all around you.

🌱

Pardon me if it seems I speak in riddles.
For I do not mean to. Riddles are obscure,
while the path to forward walking is clear—
as clear as the flowers before you.

For plants, my young friend, know a secret—
the secret to forward walking.

🌱

It seems odd to say that plants walk forward, but they do.

And it is a shame that their knowledge of
forward walking remains a secret,
for they have been speaking of it to all
who would listen, from the beginning of time.

🌱

Listen to them, my young friend,
and they will show you the way.

The Service of Plants

You can hear the secret most plainly
when you are listening from a great distance.

For the secret of plants is most obvious in plants' absence.

*

This is not another riddle
but simply recognition of what is sadly true:
man sees lack much more readily than abundance.

It is when plants are absent that we learn to see them.

*

My learning from plants began
as I wandered across a stark desert plain.

For five days I could find no relief from the heat.
Food was scarce. With no vegetation, I lived on snakes
and desert rodents, such as they were. In the barren waste
of the plain, even those creatures were scarce.

When I did find them, I ate their raw flesh,
for there was no wood to make fire.

*

I came to loathe that plain. It was a harsh, unforgiving place.

It lacked variety and natural beauty.

It provided no refuge from the heat or the storms.

It was barren of the habitats necessary
to support most creatures.

It contained very little food and lacked the wood
that would allow me to properly prepare what I could find.

On the morning of the third day,
I realized that although the plain seemed
to lack so much, it really lacked only one thing:

Vegetation.

All that I missed was the service provided by plants.

The Source of Beauty

Of all the creations of Mother Earth,
perhaps none serve so fully as the plants.

Consider their service:

They provide food, shelter, shade, habitat,
support against erosion, and raw material for the
construction of tools and preparation of fire.

Is it just a coincidence that the creations that provide
the most help happen as well to be the most beautiful?

I think not.

For I have known people who provide service
after the manner of plants, and their lives have been
the most beautiful lives I have known.

They, like the plants, reach to the heavens in their living,
and in their reaching heavenward, they have reached to me.

Counterfeits

But beware, my young friend.
There are counterfeits among nature.

Every plant that is good for food is mimicked
by another that will make you ill.

*

In this, nature teaches about life.
For there are many dangerous elements
who will try to make themselves appealing in your eyes.

Most of them will not think themselves dangerous, and the
danger is that you will not, either. They may act in ways you
find fun and exciting. And in their delivery of gratification,
you may mistake them as doing you a service.

But beware. Some oak is good, other is poison.
There are many whose offering—however enticing—
is not joy but strife.

Just as you must separate the good from
the counterfeit in nature, so must you do in your life.

*

Am I sounding old and out of touch?

I very much hope to sound old, for old I am.
And it is because of my years that I can give counsel.

But if I sound to you out of touch, I worry for your health.
I fear you may already be intoxicated by counterfeits.

I know how intoxicating counterfeits can be.
For it was under their influence that I turned my back
on all the truth in my life.

It was not until I saw poison masquerading as food
that I committed to remain on the path to recovery.

My young friend, pay attention to what you take in.
I have had many bitter years
because of the bitter fruit I have tasted.

As you learn how to discern the good and the evil in nature,
you will discover a capacity to do the same in life.

In this, too, the plants do you a service.

Hope for the Desert

In many desert regions,
there can be found a most interesting plant.

It is plain and unspectacular. For years
it languishes in obscurity, keeping close
to the earth and drawing no attention to itself.
There is nothing about it that makes it desirable.

But these many years of apparent inactivity are actually years
of preparation. Suddenly, as if from out of nowhere, the
plant thrusts a giant stalk heavenward. In one brief season,
this most humble and lowly plant grows beyond all others.

It lifts itself up so that all can see.

But then, at the height of its reputation and power,
the plant suddenly dies.

Those who do not know better would think it stricken
and afflicted. But its sudden death is according to plan.

It dies because it gives all that it has in its ascent
toward the sky. And this ascent is not in vain.
For in death, it spreads seeds of life upon the earth.
It dies that others might rise as well.

My young friend, let the century plant's life
inspire and guide you.

Speak less and learn more. Prepare yourself to stand tall
and straight. In all that you do, point heavenward.

Do so, and you will inspire others to do the same.

The dry desert slopes and asphalt expanses of your day
need your inspiring presence.

Plant yourself in good soil.
Treasure the dews from heaven and store up water
in your soul. In all your days, bask in the light of the sun.

Then you, like the century plant, will become a beacon of
hope, and for you its sacrifice won't have been in vain.

6

The Path of Animals

A Badger and a Stone

Animals sense our walking.

I don't mean merely that they know our presence. I mean
that, in moments, they sense the intentions of our hearts—
whether our hearts are walking forward or backward.

🐾

You may wonder at my saying this. There was a time
when I wouldn't have believed it myself.

But then I met a badger with a stone.

🐾

It happened not long after I escaped
the land of winding cliffs.

My moccasins had disintegrated from my feet, and with
them some of my confidence among the hills. Red ants
and stickers bade me turn around at each step. Finally,
I collapsed to rest in the pungent shade of a sagebrush.

After a few minutes, I heard from the other side
of the brush a muffled growl and spitting noise.
I turned my head to look.

Less than five feet away was a freshly dug hole.
From the hole a furry rump emerged—the rump of
a massive badger backing its way up the dirt ramp.
He held loosely in his front claws a fist-sized stone,
dragging and rolling it along up the ramp.

66

I forgot my troubles as I watched the scene.
As the badger's body topped the ramp, he pitched
awkwardly down the other side and lost hold of the stone.
He growled and went back after it. Time and time again
he attempted the same, only to lose hold at the top.
When finally he succeeded and was about to go back—
perhaps for another rock or for a rest—he saw me.

In that moment I almost fainted.
For in my interest in the badger's project,
I had forgotten how ferocious they could be.

He gave me a long look, then a nod,
and slipped smoothly down the ramp into his new den.

🐾

Old Badger sensed my heart.

I meant no harm.

In that moment, I resolved to walk peaceably
with animals in my walking.

The Language of Animals

Unfortunately, I have not always so walked.

Very often before that day, and all too often since,
I have failed to care enough about animals to learn
how to converse with them in their own languages.

☜

Yes, you heard right.
Converse with them in their own languages.

All creation speaks and listens.
It is only man that is hard of hearing.

The badger spoke to me that day by the brush,
and many creatures have spoken to me since—
the deer, the snake, the mountain lion . . .

☜

In all that you and I do, we speak to them as well,
for our movements are part of our speaking.

Faces among the Animals

I have learned that my failure to connect with animals
has been a mirror of my failure to connect with people.

The deer I have failed to appreciate,

the snake I provoked to anger,

the mountain lion I made to run in fear . . .

Look hard, my young friend, and you will see as I have—
these animals have faces, and they are faces
of people we have known.

How surprised I was to discover this. For I ran to the
wilderness to be alone. But what I discovered when
I arrived was that I brought my world with me.

It came with me because my world is how I perceive it—
and invite it to be—by my heart.

I entered the wilderness with the same bitter heart
that I carried among my people.

What I discovered—first then, and many times since—
was that everywhere we go, we bring our world with us.

The animals, by their responses to us, give us a chance to see
not just a new wilderness but, in the same act, a new home.

For our malice shows itself through them
and reveals our backward walking.

Each face before me gives me the chance to love all faces.

My young friend, do you understand my speaking?

Learn to live peaceably with the deer, the snake,
and the mountain lion, and you will discover peace
as well toward your people.

Honoring Creation

Early on, I was afraid of the animals.

But that was because I was thinking of myself.

When I learned to think of *them*, all fear left me.
In its place, I felt wonder and peace.

❀

Here is what I mean by "thinking of the animals":

When I see a deer, I wonder what her life must be like.

When I encounter a snake, I watch to learn
how he goes about finding his prey.

When I come across a mountain lion,
I observe his elusive nature and how his shyness
keeps him a rare sight among the two-legged beings.

For before I entered the wilderness, if I thought about others,
it was only to find what was wrong in them.

To find in other creatures things that are of interest,
things to appreciate, that was a new experience indeed.

❀

Soon, I found myself longing for the deer, respecting
the vital business of the snake, and learning from the
common sense of the mountain lion.

Quite naturally, simply by taking an interest in them,
I learned their languages—the sounds, actions, and smells
they respond well to, and those that trouble them.

I learned to walk peaceably among them.

Like all creations, the deer, the snake, and the mountain lion
were honored that I would respect their Belonging Place.

They accepted my walking and returned peace.

The Offering of Animals

Perhaps it surprises you to hear the word *peace* applied
to animals, since so many of them kill to survive.
But observe them and you will understand.
There are two ways to walk, even in hunting.

Let me explain with another legend—a story known
among my people as "The Legend of the Lamb."

It is said that before the foundation of the earth was laid,
the animals gathered in a grand council
to decide the order of their existence.

How could they survive and multiply? they wondered.
What would be their source of food? Would all eat grass?
Then what would be left to cover the earth in softness?
And who would inhabit the highest climbs and lowest vales?

The debate grew loud and heated.

Amid the clamor, the grand council failed to notice one among
them who had made his way slowly to the fore.

He called to them, "My brothers and sisters of the earth."

All who were talking fell silent. Before them stood one who ate
grass—a lamb. Not just any lamb, but the greatest of them all.

"My dear friends," he began. "You are dear to me, as you know.
I have come to know your hearts, each and every one.
They will lead you to multiply and replenish the earth—
from its tips to its depths. For this is the desire that is in you—
the desire to fulfill the measure of your creation.

"But you must be free to do so—the bird must fly,
the lion must roam the land, the fish must explore all the waters.

"You must not be bound to the grass.

"I will provide you the freedom you need
by providing you all with food."

The grand council looked around in wonder.
"What food?" they asked, almost in unison.

"I will offer myself as your food," he said.
"My flesh and blood will sustain you wherever you need to go."

"But how can it?" asked one.

"You will see," said he.

The grand council fell silent.

The silence continued for hours.
It was not a time for words, only for feelings.
All were pondering the sacrifice of the lamb.

Finally, out of the reverent stillness
a dove took flight and lifted a song on the wind.

"This act must not be forgotten," it sang.

"This act must be remembered still.

Our lives must join in the offering,

our acts must testify of his."

The dove lighted on the shoulder of the lamb
while the music grew on the wind.

The grand council joined in one voice and song,
adding their words to the breeze.

"We too must offer as he has done," they sang.

"We too must give,

for each act of offering

points to the act whereby life was given."

My young friend,

do you see why I use the word *peace* to describe animals?

Their deaths are sacred offerings.

They make the same gift to you and to me
as they do to their fellow creatures.

In similitude of the lamb,
they give of themselves that others might live.

7

The Path of "WE"

The Story of My People

I would like to tell you more about my people.

Our story may help you to see the world anew
and to discover the majesty that lives in the hills.

❦

My people have been upon the earth
as long as time itself, or at least so it is told.

According to legend, the Creator made Mother Earth
and dressed her with light, wind, water, stone,
plants, and animals. Then he placed my people
among his creation.

It is said that all creation lived in harmony. In all that they
did, light, wind, water, stone, plants, animals, and my
people supported one another. They had become, in the
language of my people, "WE"—that is, "as one."

This pleased the Creator.

But this harmony did not last. Some say that a dark cloud
enveloped the earth and turned my people from the path
of light. Other say they were bound by a great cord, keeping
their feet from the sure path of stone. However it happened,
the hearts of my people began to walk backward against
creation. Darkness reigned, and the harmony was broken.

Witnessing the strife among the workmanship
of his hands, the Creator shed tears as the rain upon the
mountains. Unless creation could again be made as one,
the children of Mother Earth would be lost.

According to the legend, the tears he shed were divine.
They were a manifestation of his love for man, and that love
descended from the heavens and bathed all creation.

Light, wind, water, stone, plants, and animals—all of which
had been darkened by the backward walk of my people—
were created anew. The Creator's love was made to shine
through them in ways that could cut through any darkness.

For by the Creator's act of love, the elements
had become "WE"—one in each other and in Him.

Through their unified testimony of Him,
they invited man to join them.

My View of My People

Sometime after the great rain, it is said that spirits
visited my people and taught them the path of WE.

Belief in WE—even aspiration to it—has been
a part of my people ever since. According to legend,
it is said that on occasion, some of my people
have attained the status of WE and have been taken up
into the bosom of the Creator to live out their days.

For my part, I never believed this or any other portion of
the legend. The traditions of my fathers seemed old and
irrelevant. But I couldn't escape them, for my parents
believed, and their parents before them, and the idea of WE,
as I mentioned earlier, was built into our very language.

𓃢

As my heart turned from my people,
I began to walk backward, and to stumble
over their traditions, beliefs, and expectations.

My people and their ways appeared backward to me.

"WE appear as WE are," my father told me—or, in your
language, "Others appear as we ourselves are."

But by then my heart had walked too far away to hear him.

I had already rejected my people.

Awakening to WE

When I entered the wilderness,
I was determined to show my people wrong.

I was committed to learning nothing among nature
except for the foolishness of my fathers.

So began my education in WE.

🦶

Yes, WE. Did you think it foolish the way
I described the traditions of my people?

I was the one who was foolish.
And it was nature that taught me so.

For the wind taught me that we *are* connected,
just as the elders among my people had suggested.

Stone taught me that I continually wield influence on others
around me—inviting them toward peace or toward war.

Plants recalled to my memory the peaceful offerings
I had received from my people, while encounters with
animals revealed just how much my invitation
to others had been toward war.

Water purified my memory and brought me to my home.
And light chased away the darkness and revealed in all
around me the Creator of all.

You may not believe in divine tears or in redeeming
power that descended below all things so that creation
could be reclaimed from darkness.

But know this, my young friend: in the wilderness,
I was reclaimed from darkness. And I have met many
along my way who have been reclaimed as well.

Walk among the hills, the trees, the valleys,
and the streams, and you will know in your heart
that independence is a myth.

For "I" stands connected to others in WE.

To be alive is to be with others.

To be at peace with others is to be WE.

The Lie in the "I"

My young friend, you live in the age of the "I,"
and the age is taking its toll.

As I mentioned earlier, modern man looks out for
himself and only secondarily for others. He is consumed
with satisfying his own personal "needs."

Ironically, man's obsession with personal
wants has obscured his greatest need—
the need to live in harmony with others.

🐾

Listen to your heart, and it will verify my words.

You and I *have* needs, of course, but to recognize
that we do is to recognize that others have them as well.
Human needs do not divide us, as your day suggests.
Rather, they *unite* us. For we are each of us equally needy.

To see another clearly is to see someone
very much like yourself.

🐾

So when others seem very different from you—when they
seem irritating, maddening, and troubling, and you are
bothered by them—the path of WE would invite you,
as the elders among my people invited me, to consider
how *you* might be irritating, maddening, and troubling.

After all, when I first cursed at the wilderness,

I thought that I cursed it because it was a cursed place.

But my cursing was a lie, as I have since discovered.
My cursings were never about the wilderness at all.

The wilderness just happened to get in the way
of a *heart* that was cursing.

My young friend, walk forward and you will see others
one way. Walk backward and you will see them another.
The way you choose to see others depends
on the direction of your heart.

So in all that you see, think, and feel about others,
remember—

We are all connected.

"WE [others] appear as WE [ourselves] are."

To see another is to see one's self.

The Creed of WE

To see the first truth of WE—
that all is connected—is to see the second:
that there is purpose in the order of things.

🦶

Light, wind, water, stone, plants, and animals
combine to make a beautiful creation.

But the outer world is only a representation of the inner.

Light brightens more than the landscape, wind speaks to
more than the trees, water cleanses more than the body.

The creation of the earth points to the creation of a soul.

🦶

In my walking, I have learned to ponder both creations.
And Mother Earth has been generous in the
lessons she has taught me.

These are the truths she has spoken:

Look for light.

Listen for inspiration on the wind.

Let water cleanse your soul.

Set yourself on a firm foundation.

Serve as the plants.

Sacred offerings ?

Do not offend your fellow creatures.

Live in harmony with all creation.

🦶

This, my young friend, is the most sacred of
rememberings to carry in your heart.

Do so, and the awakenings from the wilderness
will accompany you wherever you walk.

🦶

Wherever you walk, you will walk well
if you walk on the path of WE.

The path of WE will return you to your true self and
to your Belonging Place among your people.

Destinations

Forward Walking

Lone Walking

I shall forever be grateful for the time
I spent alone among nature.

For clear skies helped to clear my mind.

Fresh breezes helped to freshen my soul.

Pure waters helped to purify my heart.

☽

It took hills, trees, valleys, and streams to teach
me the truth about myself and my people.

☽

For years afterward, there were times when I walked
backward in embarrassment, self-pity, and pride.

Grace ☽ *Forgiving Nature*

Regardless, light patiently shone from above, stone kept
supporting me from beneath, wind still lent me breath.

Water gave me drink, vegetation provided me protection,
and animals offered their flesh for food.

The Creator lengthened my days, and in each of those days,
nature humbly showed me how I hadn't been,
and could yet be, with my people.

After many years, this humility was finally able
to penetrate a barrier even as thick as my pride.

The rain of the great storm led me
to the entrance of the lands of my youth.

And there, a dream finished what light, wind, and rain
had started.

The Step to a New Life

When the heavens stopped beating on me and the sky
finally cleared, I collapsed to the earth in exhaustion.

How long I slept I do not know. It might have
been hours or it might have been days.
But I did not rest in my sleep. I walked far.

And I awoke desiring to step anew.

For in my sleep I met a legend among my people—
a man long revered, with a name so sacred
it is spoken only in praise or song.

In my dream, I climbed the slope of a mountain.
My father climbed with me. I did not know the purpose
of our journey, but it appeared as if he did.

I say "appeared" because we didn't speak. We walked in
silence, although not the warring kind I had known in my
youth. It was rather the silence of reverence.

After what seemed like both a long time and barely a
moment, we reached the summit. My father stopped,
and with an outstretched arm he invited me
to proceed beyond the next bend.

I did as I was bidden.

As I turned the corner, I was overcome by the
presence of an incredible being—a being that
I instinctively knew to be the holy one from our legends.

I recall that he was in some sort of conversation with another person. But he turned toward me, and I was given to know that he was waiting specifically for me.

He radiated an incredible light, yet the light was neither blinding nor harsh. It was inviting, soft, and loving. Nevertheless, it was bright beyond description.

I felt in that moment love as I had never known it. It drew me to him. I rushed to him and we embraced. I think that I fell at his feet, but I can no longer remember for sure. I shall never forget that embrace, however, nor his eyes, for they were pure love.

But amid the glory of the experience, there was an element that left me troubled. For while I knew by instinct that I was in the arms of the holy one, I remember wondering while we were embracing whether it really was him.

In that moment of uncertainty, I knew that something in the way I had been living my life held me back from experiencing his fullness, and my heart shuddered in anguish.

Then I awoke.

My young friend, I wish you were near me so that you could see the conviction in my eyes and hear the feeling in my voice.

I truly saw what I have described to you. It was a dream, yes, but so much more of a dream than any other dream I have known.

I had never before experienced such joy
and had never before felt such pain.

When I had collected my thoughts, I lifted my voice to the sky, thanking the Creator that I had been given another day to leave behind what had held me back.

For you see, I was carrying in my heart rememberings of a life lived in backward walking.

If I was to move forward,
I needed to leave all that was backward behind.

Perhaps in this regard, as well, you and I are alike. Perhaps there are aspects of your life that need to be started anew.

Whatever you carry that invites a backward walking, leave it behind.

I did that on that very day.

I have had to repeat the offering many times since.

Make an offering of all that is old within you.

For the embrace that awaits is too sweet to miss.

Together Walking

I speak of not only the embrace of my dream
but the embraces of this world as well.

For my failure to fully embrace the holy one was
a type and shadow of my failure to embrace my people.

�☌

I told myself that I had *reason* to hold back from them.
After all, they had done wrong.

But the holy one replaced my logic
with his love. For he took me in his arms
despite all the wrongs *I* had done.

☌

I shall ever remember the day I descended Big Mountain
to walk again among my people.

It was a warm summer day, and the sun shone high
in the sky. Children were playing the games of our people—
the games I had loved in my youth.

The smell of roasted venison greeted my senses and brought
with it warm memories of feasts from the past.

☌

My family lived in a humble home
on the opposite side of the village.

I had so much to say and no idea how to say it. I had stayed
three days on the slopes of the mountain trying to prepare
my speaking. But every preparation seemed wrong.
I felt moved to go and speak purely from my heart.

☊

I saw my father first. He was frailer than I remembered—
more bent, more weathered.

I came up from behind him as he struggled to move a log.

"Father," I said, with more respect than
I had ever heard in my own voice, "can WE help WE?"

He turned to me and froze, as if trying
to recognize the image before him.

Then his eyes welled with tears, his body softened,
and we fell into each other's arms.

☊

This embrace was followed by many others
as I began a new walking with my family.

Life became sweeter than I had ever dreamed it could be.

☊

Don't misunderstand. All walkers sometimes stumble.
Sometimes, despite all I have seen, heard, and felt, I have
nevertheless withheld myself from their embraces.

But every time I have seen the dawn, or felt a breeze,
or drunk from a stream, or walked on a stone, or
eaten of a plant, or looked upon a lamb,
I have been reminded again of the truth:

My feet were placed on Mother Earth in the midst of others'
so that I might learn to walk together with them in my heart.

You and I, my young friend, walk only as far and
as well as our hearts walk among our people.

Words to a Friend

I now bid you farewell.

I wish I could see you and you could see me.
I wish we could look together at the night sky and
drink together from the same mountain stream.
I wish I could take you into my arms and let you feel
the truth and joy that it took me so long to know.

My words will be all that you know of me.

I offer them to you in peace, in the hope that perhaps
you will discover within you and in the world around you
a Guide who will lead you home.

Listen closely and you will hear whisperings.

Follow them, and eventually you will discover
a voice so distinct in its peaceful stillness that it will cut
through the noise of the most confusing days.

I know this voice. I have learned to stay close to it
and to feel when I am pulling away. Time after time
in my walking, it has returned me to my people.

Mercifully, despite my weaknesses and stumblings,
all now is as it should be.

Is all as it should be for you?

That is my question for you, dear friend.

Perhaps you have your own mountain to descend
or village to cross.

And perhaps someone *you* have left awaits an embrace.

If so, you are fortunate indeed.

For those you need are still with you.

I now lift my voice to the Creator in your behalf,
that you might have courage where you need it.

That you might be blessed by light, by wind, by rain.

That you might learn from stone, plant, and lamb.

That all creation might work for your healing.

That you might embrace all you have left.

This is my desire for your walking, dear friend.

That you, too, will discover a people.

And with them, the joy of **We**.

About the Art

WE do not fight WE.

 The two figures are warriors. The line between the two warriors shows the break in their relationship, or the break in the unity of WE. The dead animal below is the catalyst of the break.

Light chases away darkness.

 LIGHT: The sun above the figure symbolizes a source of light that is always present. The figure is touching the light. This signifies that light is not only seen but, more importantly, can be felt within. *Left side:* The shaded lines represent the light being obscured. The bottom-jagged rays represent a hazardous path in the darkness, or backward walking. *Right side:* The rays of light are clean and straight. This symbolizes forward walking and the happiness that is found in the light. The overall shape of this hieroglyph resembles a larger figure with the sun as the head. That figure represents the source of light, or the Creator.

For our hearts are ever sending messages on the wind.

 WIND: In this drawing the lines on each side represent wind. The two lines represent two senses: feeling and smell. Even though we cannot see the wind, it still exists. The wind can be felt and smelled. Wind is connected to us and leads our presence before we arrive. This connection can be seen in this figure. *Left side:* The wind moving downward depicts backward walking, or movement away from progress. *Right side:* The wind rises, showing ascension or progression. Forward walking brings us closer to the Creator and elevates all Two-Legged beings (humans).

Water, too, is a gift from above.

 WATER: The three half circles represent the clouds, the heavens, and the living water—or Creator. The lines coming from the clouds represent rain. The lines below the figure symbolize a body of water like a river. *Left side:* This shows backward walking. The water is jagged, which represents danger and toxicity. The clouds do not cross to the left; a line replaces them instead. This line represents drought. *Right side:* Four lines descend from the clouds and touch different parts of the figure. Where they connect is important in this depiction. Rain nourishes our mind (the head), softens the heart (the chest), shapes our doing (the hand), and clears our path (the foot). The source of our existence is water.

Do we invite peace or provoke war?

 STONE: The lines on each side represent an extension of ourselves and the paths that we create—toward peace or toward war. *Left side:* The two jagged lines represent an unpredictable and hazardous path. The shape below the lines is a stone turned upside down. The footing on that stone is unsteady. Notice that the stone is black. This represents a dark and encumbered path. *Right side:* The stone is right side up, showing stable and sure footing. The two lines represent a straight path, or forward walking. The movement is upward, symbolizing progression.

As you learn to discern the good and the evil in nature, you will discover a capacity to do the same in life.

 **PLANTS:** The symbol above the figure is the sun. The sun is necessary for plants and all of creation. The figure of the man is connected to a plant on the left and right. This is to denote the connection we have to all plants. The connection shows

that even toxic plants can have a proper use. The hands connected to the plants symbolize the help that plants continually offer. *Left side:* The plant is jagged and will hurt anyone who holds it. It is also upside down. This means that the plant is toxic and will cause confusion and damage. *Right side:* The plant is healthy and gives life. It reaches upward, toward the light, and is fruitful.

Their deaths are sacred offerings.

 ANIMALS: A line connects each animal to the figure. This shows our connection to animals: their sacrifice, companionship, and beauty—and the way they offer us life. It is what we do with those offerings that will honor or disrespect the animal. *Left side:* This shows backward walking. The animal is upside down, representing a dead animal. The antler is dark, representing an encumbered path. The dead, upside-down animal depicts a failure to see its sacrifice. *Right side:* The animal is right side up and leading the way forward. The upward animal shows that we keep the animals alive in our minds and "doings." We honor their lives and offerings. The horn represents the path of the journey. It is clear and unencumbered.

To be alive is to be with others.

 Path of WE: The original figures are found on ancient pottery. They depict a tribe or community living in harmony. On ancient pottery each figure is connected: They stand side by side, holding hands all the way around the pot. There is no beginning or end. Holding hands is symbolic of unity, survival, and a commitment to each other and to life. The arrows on the end of the hands on this figure signify the continuation of that unity. The male and female warriors show people standing solidly together to protect one another in the battle between good and evil. The warriors represent us.

Acknowledgments

First and foremost, we acknowledge the hand of the Creator in the writing of this book. It is He who guided Larry Olsen to the hills, presented Ezekiel Sanchez (Good Buffalo Eagle) the dreams, gave Pauline Martin Sanchez (Gentle White Dove), a Navajo tribal member, the language of the Ancient Ones, and put the narrative into the heart of James Ferrell.

When Larry was twelve years old, he found an obsidian arrowhead in his uncle's field. His find sparked a lifelong quest to learn and replicate the primitive technologies of the ancient peoples who had walked the land before him. In the early 1960s, Larry began teaching outdoor survival classes. In 1968, he led his first thirty-day expedition. To his surprise, the students not only found value in learning the skills but also reported making profound changes in their lives after applying the simple truths they had learned living primitively among nature.

Among these students was a young Totonac Indian from Mexico named Ezekiel. When Ezekiel was a child, his responsibility was to capture small game and gather wild edibles to help feed his father's large family. He spent his youth working in the migrant fields until the age of nineteen. Larry immediately noticed his familiarity with nature and asked Ezekiel to join him. This was the start of a long and trusted friendship. Larry and Ezekiel developed a university course, which in 1969 won a National Education Award: "Youth Rehabilitation through Outdoor Survival."

Over the next several years, thousands of students participated in courses that Larry and Ezekiel developed. In 1988, Larry asked Ezekiel to join him in the creation of "ANASAZI Foundation, the Making of a Walking." Pondering the invitation, Ezekiel was given two dreams. The first dream is being fulfilled today through the work of the foundation. The second dream begins with the publishing of this book.

Ezekiel's wife, Pauline, assisted in the creation of ANASAZI's early curriculum, which centered around seven elements found in nature. They called this "The Seven Paths of the ANASAZI Way." In 1989, Larry, Ezekiel, and Pauline became acquainted with Dr. C. Terry Warner, a professor of philosophy and founder of the Arbinger Institute. Fascinated by their work, Dr. Warner later commissioned James Ferrell, a scholar and his former student, to put "The Seven Paths of the ANASAZI Way" into a narrative account.

Our heartfelt thanks to you, James Ferrell, Dr. Warner, and the Arbinger Institute, for your gracious gifts and commitment to merge the philosophy and vision of ANASAZI into a narrative that is helping countless hearts to "walk forward in the light."

We also acknowledge the incredible people who have worked with us over these many years. With recognition to Bob Gay, Lester Moore, Paul Smith and Sterling Tanner, without which ANASAZI would not have survived difficult times. We can do little more than bow down before you in gratitude for the sacrifices you have made and for how you have touched our lives.

Also deserving mention are the many generous contributors who have given much to further the work of ANASAZI. Of special mention: Sherrell Olsen, Susan Warner, Gaylene Merchant, Lynette Gay, Brenda Tanner, Jeanie Moore, Lyn Smith, Stephen R. Covey, Barbara Bush, Steve and Barb Young, Forever Young Foundation, Wynonna Judd, Marie Osmond, Dale Tingey, Richard and Mimi Peery, Tom and Jan Lewis, Bob and Diana Hunt, Thom and Gail Williamsen, the Sorensen Legacy Fund, Mac and Susan Dunwoody, Wayne and Connie Greene, Ross and Anita Farnsworth, Marc and Angela Tahiliani, Harry Tahiliani, Dinah Lundell, Richard Ferre, Rich and Krista Haws, and Ralph and Glenda Earle.

To Lehi Sanchez (Thunder Voice Eagle), we thank you for the beautiful art in this book.

And a last word of acknowledgment goes to Seth Adam Smith, who gave a worn copy of the original manuscript to the wonderful team at Berrett-Koehler Publishers and diligently worked for its publication. And to Jeevan Sivasubramaniam, managing director, Editorial, who read it and believed.

—Michael J. Merchant

President, ANASAZI Foundation

About ANASAZI Foundation

ANASAZI
FOUNDATION

In the Native American tradition, life is a "walking." One's walking is determined by the state of one's heart toward all that is around him. *Anasazi* is a Navajo word commonly interpreted as "the Ancient Ones." According to legends, the wise teachers taught that the Creator placed man on the earth in order for him to learn how to "walk forward"—in harmony with man and all creation.

For years, ANASAZI Foundation—a nonprofit 501(c)(3) organization headquartered in Arizona—has served families by introducing them to a New Beginning and helping them to discover their Seed of Greatness and the wisdom of the lives led by these Ancient Ones.

Founded by renowned wilderness pioneers Larry Olsen and Ezekiel Sanchez, ANASAZI gives young people an opportunity, through a primitive living experience and a philosophy that invites healing at the hands of nature, to effect a change of heart—a change in one's whole way of walking in the world. ANASAZI's wilderness experience is nonpunitive. To those at ANASAZI, the wilderness is not a harsh place to break youth down but rather a safe place—a place free from distractions, where one can learn, ponder, discover, and build.

Through this experience and ANASAZI's concurrent work with parents, ANASAZI prepares parents and children to turn their hearts to one another, begin anew, and walk in harmony in the wilderness of the world.

ANASAZI Foundation, (800) 678-3445, www.anasazi.org

From the Arbinger Institute—Inspired in part by
their work with ANASAZI Foundation

The Anatomy of Peace
Resolving the Heart of Conflict

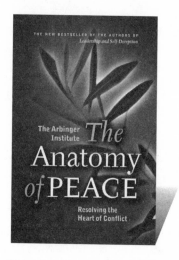

Through an intriguing story of parents struggling with their
troubled children and with their own personal problems, *The
Anatomy of Peace* shows how to get past the preconceived ideas
and self-justifying reactions that keep us from seeing the world
clearly and dealing with it effectively.

Along with the parents, we meet Yusuf al-Falah, an Arab, and Avi
Rozen, a Jew, each of whom lost his father at the hands of the
other's ethnic cousins. As the story unfolds, we discover how they
came together, how they help warring parents and children come
together, and how we too can find our way out of the struggles
that weigh us down.

Hardcover, 256 pages, ISBN 978-1-57675-334-7
Paperback, ISBN 978-1-57675-584-6
PDF ebook, ISBN 978-1-57675-955-4

BK° Berrett–Koehler Publishers, Inc.
San Francisco, *www.bkconnection.com*   **800.929.2929**

✷ Berrett–Koehler
BK̄ Publishers

Berrett-Koehler is an independent publisher dedicated to an ambitious mission: *Creating a World That Works for All.*

We believe that to truly create a better world, action is needed at all levels—individual, organizational, and societal. At the individual level, our publications help people align their lives with their values and with their aspirations for a better world. At the organizational level, our publications promote progressive leadership and management practices, socially responsible approaches to business, and humane and effective organizations. At the societal level, our publications advance social and economic justice, shared prosperity, sustainability, and new solutions to national and global issues.

A major theme of our publications is "Opening Up New Space." Berrett-Koehler titles challenge conventional thinking, introduce new ideas, and foster positive change. Their common quest is changing the underlying beliefs, mindsets, institutions, and structures that keep generating the same cycles of problems, no matter who our leaders are or what improvement programs we adopt.

We strive to practice what we preach—to operate our publishing company in line with the ideas in our books. At the core of our approach is stewardship, which we define as a deep sense of responsibility to administer the company for the benefit of all of our "stakeholder" groups: authors, customers, employees, investors, service providers, and the communities and environment around us.

We are grateful to the thousands of readers, authors, and other friends of the company who consider themselves to be part of the "BK Community." We hope that you, too, will join us in our mission.

A BK Life Book

This book is part of our BK Life series. BK Life books change people's lives. They help individuals improve their lives in ways that are beneficial for the families, organizations, communities, nations, and world in which they live and work. To find out more, visit **www.bk-life.com**.

Berrett–Koehler
Publishers

A community dedicated to creating
a world that works for all

Visit Our Website: www.bkconnection.com

Read book excerpts, see author videos and Internet movies, read
our authors' blogs, join discussion groups, download book apps, find
out about the BK Affiliate Network, browse subject-area libraries of
books, get special discounts, and more!

Subscribe to Our Free E-Newsletter, the *BK Communiqué*

Be the first to hear about new publications, special discount offers,
exclusive articles, news about bestsellers, and more! Get on the list
for our free e-newsletter by going to **www.bkconnection.com**.

Get Quantity Discounts

Berrett-Koehler books are available at quantity discounts for orders
of ten or more copies. Please call us toll-free at (800) 929-2929 or
email us at bkp.orders@aidcvt.com.

Join the BK Community

BKcommunity.com is a virtual meeting place where people from
around the world can engage with kindred spirits to create a world
that works for all. BKcommunity.com members may create their own
profiles, blog, start and participate in forums and discussion groups,
post photos and videos, answer surveys, announce and register for
upcoming events, and chat with others online in real time. Please join
the conversation!